MW00423385

ROWING TO AMERICA: The Immigrant Project

A Collection of Nine One-act Plays

Commissioned by the
Playwrights Theatre of New Jersey

Dead Bolivians on a Raft by Guillermo Reyes
The Apron by Meg Griffith
Rowing to America by Kitty Chen
Slave Coffle w/ Observer by J. Rufus Caleb
Homeland by Sachi Oyama
Famous Ali by Robert Clyman
A Mule in J.F.K. by Keith Glover
Let Us Go Then by Akhil Sharma
Oh Wild West Wind by Karen Sunde

Dramatic Publishing
Woodstock, Illinois • London, England • Melbourne, Australia

*** NOTICE ***

©MCMXCIX by
PLAYWRIGHTS THEATRE OF NEW JERSEY

Printed in the United States of America
All Rights Reserved
(ROWING TO AMERICA: The Immigrant Project)

ISBN 0-87129-902-X

IMPORTANT BILLING AND CREDIT REQUIREMENTS

Playwrights Theatre
gratefully acknowledges Kitty Chen
for the use of her title "Rowing to America."

ROWING TO AMERICA:
The Immigrant Project

A Collection of Nine One-act Plays
For 5 Men and 5 Women
(Ages range from late teens to mid-50s.)

Contents

ROWING TO AMERICA: The Immigrant Project was commissioned by and premiered at the Playwrights Theatre of New Jersey in 1997, John Pietrowski, Producing Artistic Director, and Joseph Megel, Artistic Director. The production included the following artists:

DEAD BOLIVIANS ON A RAFT
By Guillermo Reyes
Directed by Joseph Giardina

Gulliver	ISAIAH CAZARES
Manuel	MILES GROSE
Rigoberta	DIVINA COOK

THE APRON
By Meg Griffith
Directed by Brian Platt

Maire McMahon	MILLIE CHOW
Peig McMahon	TIFFANY MARSHALL

ROWING TO AMERICA
By Kitty Chen
Directed by John Pietrowski

Girl	MILLIE CHOW
Sister	FELICIA WILSON

SLAVE COFFLE W/ OBSERVER
By J. Rufus Caleb
Directed by John Pietrowski

Clara .... FELICIA WILSON
Charles............................... EDDIE ALDRIDGE
Observer .... TIFFANY MARSHALL
Interviewer .... MILES GROSE

HOMELAND
By Sachi Oyama
Directed by Joseph Giardina

Keiko............................... MILLIE CHOW
Neighbor Lomeli/Student .... TAMIR
High-Tech Neighbor/Student.............. RIZWAN MANJI
Storekeeper/Student .... JAY PALIT
Other Students .... DIVINA COOK, FELICIA WILSON
       ISAIAH CAZARES, TIFFANY MARSHALL, MILES GROSE

FAMOUS ALI
By Robert Clyman
Directed by John Pietrowski

Harris................................. EDDIE ALDRIDGE
Ali....................................... RIZWAN MANJI
Latoya .... FELICIA WILSON

A MULE IN J.F.K.
by Keith Glover
Directed by Joseph Megel

Guard................................. EDDIE ALDRIDGE
Ramon............................... MILES GROSE

LET US GO THEN
By Akhil Sharma
Directed by Joseph Megel

Arjun.................................. JAY PALIT
Swati................................... TAMIR
Vijay.................................. RIZWAN MANJI

OH WILD WEST WIND
By Karen Sunde
Directed by Joseph Megel

Eda...................................... DIVINA COOK
Dawn................................ MILLIE CHOW
Red.................................. ISAIAH CAZARES

ROWING TO AMERICA:
The Immigrant Project

DEAD BOLIVIANS ON A RAFT
by Guillermo Reyes

CHARACTERS:

GULLIVER, 16, young budding playwright
MANUEL, 35, his father, Salvadoran immigrant
RIGOBERTA, 30s, his mother

SETTING: *Watts, South Central neighborhood of Los Angeles.*

AT RISE: *Early Saturday afternoon. Enter GULLIVER with his mother, RIGOBERTA.*

GULLIVER. He just wasn't talking to me, Ma.
RIGOBERTA. What did you do?
GULLIVER. Nothing, I just— *(Hesitates.)* I—I better—
RIGOBERTA. Ya pues, dime! *(Say it!)*
GULLIVER. I'm writing a play.
RIGOBERTA. Oh...like a Passion Play?
GULLIVER. Well, it is for the church, but—
RIGOBERTA. Yes, a religious play. Que bien!
GULLIVER. Not really, you see— My creative writing teacher told Father Guido that I'm just about the best student in—
RIGOBERTA. Oye, be more humble. La humildad, mijo, humbleness goes a long way.
GULLIVER *(a little intimidated)*. I'm sorry, I meant the teacher told the priest that I might be able in a very

11

modest fashion to entertain the humble masses in our spring festival because I'm so extremely talented—in a very modest way—and then I think Dad found out—

RIGOBERTA. But Papi would be very proud of you, mijo. La comunidad needs more boys like you doing such nice, useless things like plays—

GULLIVER. Sure thing, Ma, but you see...I think Dad found out it's an immigrant play and he—

RIGOBERTA. What's wrong with that?

GULLIVER. You don't understand, it's an "illegal alien" play.

RIGOBERTA. As long as you don't mention names—

GULLIVER. I do mention names, I mention everybody, I mention all of you.

RIGOBERTA. Oh!

(MANUEL enters, they all freeze.)

MANUEL. Okay, we have to talk, de hombre a hombre, cara a cara.

GULLIVER. I'll change the names, that was just the first draft, I'll make sure they become citizens by the end of page ten. *(Sees script in his dad's hand.)* Wait... how did you get a copy of the script?

MANUEL. At the church.

GULLIVER. They're passing them out?

RIGOBERTA. We're gonna be in trouble! *(To GUL-LIVER.)* Oh, sure, since you're the citizen, you don't care if the rest of us—

MANUEL. No, calmate, vieja! Nobody's gonna get in trouble! They were having auditions at the church, they wanted community actors, and I just wanted to know how come he, my own son, didn't tell me about it?

GULLIVER. You?

RIGOBERTA. Si, pues, you?!

GULLIVER. Dad, you're not a—

MANUEL. It says right here, "Manuel is a Salvadoran father who escaped the war and now is settled in Watts." That sounds like me, I should be able to play him.

GULLIVER. Dad...I want a real actor!

RIGOBERTA. You can't turn down your own father! He'll work for cheap.

GULLIVER. I want to maintain some professional standards.

MANUEL. I did *Streetcar Llamado Deseo* in San Salvador Community Theater, remember, vieja, you were Blanca Du Bois.

RIGOBERTA. Shut up, that was my "wild" period, don't need to remind anyone.

MANUEL. I threw you across the room, and made passionate love to you—Stanley and Blanche run away together and join the Salvadoran rebels—a little reinterpretation there.

RIGOBERTA. At the end, I got to say, "Siempre he dependido de la kindness of strangers."

GULLIVER. In Spanglish?

RIGOBERTA. Oh, you know what I mean.

MANUEL. See? This bring back good memories!

RIGOBERTA *(embarrassed)*. That's in the past, okay? But, just wondering, is there a part for the mother in this immigrant play?

GULLIVER. I'm sorry, but she's dead.

RIGOBERTA. Dead?

MANUEL. You're a ghost in this one.

RIGOBERTA. Un fantasma? I don't approve of this.

GULLIVER. It was supposed to be a surprise, you're ruining the end!

RIGOBERTA. Is she a sexy ghost? Can I wear my party dress?

GULLIVER. Please, stop it! I can't have you do my *Immigrant Ghost Sonata*—you're too close to it.

MANUEL. Are you telling us we can't try out for your own play?

RIGOBERTA. I bet he's gonna cast some gringos in it like *House of the Spirits.*

GULLIVER. Maybe I will!

RIGOBERTA. If we try out, and we get the part fair and square, por que no?

MANUEL. That's right. Don't tell us we're no good enough for you.

GULLIVER. I didn't say that! Look, okay, but only if you try out like everybody else, and let the director, Father Guido, make the final decision.

MANUEL. Then you help us prepare for the audition.

GULLIVER. I can't do that.

RIGOBERTA. Why not, se puede saber, uh?

GULLIVER. That would be giving you an unfair advantage.

RIGOBERTA. I washed cloth diapers for you.

MANUEL. I climbed mountains and deserts.

GULLIVER. I don't care if you went through Civil War for me, which you did, of course, but this is a principle—

RIGOBERTA. Never mind you. *(Turns to MANUEL.)* You explain it to me, mi amor.

MANUEL. They're on a boat, you see.

RIGOBERTA. Oh, how nice, a vacation.

MANUEL. No, they're Cubans.

RIGOBERTA. Ay, the Cuban accent is so hard.

MANUEL. No, all you do is cut out the s's—like, "oiga, cuando e' que vamo'a llega a lo E'ta'o Uni'do?" See?

RIGOBERTA. "Mira, alla 'ta Miami." Like that?

MANUEL. Very good, mi amor!

GULLIVER. Stop it! You're making fun of it all! This is a serious tragedy. Don't you understand? They're all Cubans on a raft, and they're about to discover they're all dead!

RIGOBERTA. Santa Maria! Why?

MANUEL. Manuel is alive.

GULLIVER. You don't know you're dead yet. Look, it's an abstract play. It's a surrealistic piece in a post-expressionist mode. And it's obvious you don't understand my concept, so you shouldn't try out for the play.

RIGOBERTA. And if they're dead, they can't be illegal.

MANUEL. I won't do it without changes.

GULLIVER. Not one word gets changed without my permission!

RIGOBERTA. Wait. Why can't they be Bolivians?

GULLIVER. Bolivians? They're landlocked, you can't be on a raft going to the United States all the way from Bolivia if they don't have an ocean.

MANUEL. You listen to your mother, it's a statement, dead Bolivians on a raft going to America!

GULLIVER. I won't change a thing!

MANUEL. Come here, Gulliver! Do you know how you got your name?

GULLIVER. You read *Gulliver's Travels* a hundred times in the Disney Edition, it was your favorite book when you were little.

MANUEL. And what else?

GULLIVER. It inspired you to go off and see the world. You were going to study geography, and maybe read all of Jonathan Swift in the original English...but then instead, here you are, never finished your studies, never done much of anything except loading and unloading for Don Tito's Rasquachi Market all day long, and that's fine. You pay the rent, your son gets to become the great scholar. Is that how it goes?

MANUEL. Yes, but now one day, today, the opportunity come along: the Watts Spring Festival, and I could end up starring in my own son's play about immigrants. So you really want to take away this chance from your own father?

RIGOBERTA. And from your own mother who's had to cross borders just for you?

MANUEL. And of course at the end of this new version, the family get their papers straightened out...

RIGOBERTA. And instead of being dead, could they put a down payment on a mortgage?

GULLIVER. No, they can't!

MANUEL. Son, your play must answer the one question every immigrant want to know:

GULLIVER. What?

MANUEL. How long will it take to become Republicans?

GULLIVER. Republicans?!?

RIGOBERTA. Yeah, we can't be liberals forever.

MANUEL. Will you or will you not make the changes necessary for your father and your mother to get the part just like that? Make the English a little easier to say, for instance?

RIGOBERTA. Throw in a little more Spanish, too.

GULLIVER. Well, if it means so much to you. It was a simple little play, now it's a statement.

RIGOBERTA. Si o no!

GULLIVER. Yes! Yes! You convince me, I'll never write anything that could possibly stand in your way of becoming members of the Establishment ever again!

MANUEL. Muy bien.

RIGOBERTA. We are proud of you, mijo. And, oye, make the mother a petite, I'm sick of all these humble Virgin Mary types. I want to see sexy Latina mothers on stage.

GULLIVER. I'll do my best ... *(As he exits.)* Compromises! *(GULLIVER exits.)*

RIGOBERTA. And now, my love, a ensayar!

MANUEL. We rehearse all night long. At last, we'll get to see something about us on stage, the way we want it—

RIGOBERTA. The papers get fixed!

MANUEL. They become legal residents—

RIGOBERTA. They become citizens!

MANUEL. They own a house!

RIGOBERTA. They vote for tax cuts.

MANUEL. They get to look down on new immigrants.

RIGOBERTA. They become American! *(They hug in a strange sort of "happy ending.")*

END

THE APRON
by Meg Griffith

CHARACTERS:

MAIRE McMAHON, early 20s
PEIG McMAHON, late 20s

SETTING: *The western shore of County Clare, Ireland. The year is 1870.*

AT RISE: *MAIRE wears an apron and a heavy shawl and sits on a huge rock facing the audience as she looks out to the Atlantic. Smooth stones litter the ground around her feet. PEIG, her shawl pulled about her, enters, sees MAIRE, and approaches.*

PEIG. So here you are, Maire.

MAIRE. Peig, go back to bed.

PEIG. When I woke up to put turf on the fire, you weren't in your bed. I knew you'd be down here by the water. It's where you always come. *(Pause.)* You don't have to go, Maire. I know we all gave you a big party of farewell, but all you have to do is say you want to stay.

MAIRE. Stay?

PEIG. Say you've changed your mind.

MAIRE. Stay?!

PEIG. The same people said farewell just a few hours ago will be lining up to welcome you back!

MAIRE. They love a good party, don't you know?

PEIG. They will!

MAIRE. Go back to bed, Peig.

PEIG. You won't listen, will you? *(No response.)* All right, all right. I've said all I will. Can I sit with you, then?

MAIRE. If you won't say another word. *(PEIG sits beside her. She is silent a few moments, but then cannot contain herself.)*

PEIG. You'll take a chill down here. *(MAIRE turns away from her.)* Look, your feet are getting all wet and muddy.

MAIRE. I have my shawl. I'm warm enough. My shoes will dry by the fire. You're not my mother, you know.

PEIG. Only your sister. Your *older* sister. I...I have concerns, Maire.

MAIRE. Nothing bad will happen. I keep telling you that.

PEIG. Why are you so sure about things? You've never stepped outside this county in your life and now you're taking to leave for good. But you're sure nothing bad will happen. How do you know?

MAIRE. I'm taking a boat trip in the morning. That's all I'm doing. Think of it like that.

PEIG. But—!

MAIRE. There'll be plenty of others just like me. Plenty of them. And there'll be old ones and young ones. Oh, it'll be a great adventure. I've waited all my life for such a day. How could I be afraid?

PEIG. But what about the letters? You've read them yourself.

MAIRE. People with a *little* imagination tellin' people with *no* imagination things they shouldn't be saying. I don't believe them, Peig. Those letters—carefully chosen for our eyes—are lies, all lies. They don't want us to know what it's really like to go away from this place. It's like they used to tell us about the faeries coming to snatch us away from our cradles. Why did they tell us those stories? To make us happy? To lull us to sleep? To keep us in our beds, that's why. To keep us from wandering about. They still don't want us wandering about, now, do they? They don't want us to know what we might find out there in the world. Why, if we did know, the whole island would tip over, what with all the people rushing to the west to hop into their boats to go to America!

PEIG *(laughing)*. Maire, listen to you!

MAIRE. It would, I swear! Right into the sea! *Letters*! They're trying to scare me away from going with them letters. They're trying to make me stay. I don't believe a word. Peig, there's nothing here no more. And I'm not talking just about the land or the fact we can't feed ourselves no more. There's nothing here.

PEIG. We're afraid we'll never see you again. You'll be like all the others steppin' westward. They don't come back, you know. Only Paddy Feeney come back.

MAIRE. And he not worth the missing.

PEIG. Maire!

MAIRE. Paddy Feeney. I won't be another Paddy Feeney. I promise on my grandmother's bones! Did you hear him tonight? Drunk and wailing to the heavens, he was. And everyone nodding and giving him blessings for coming back! "Poor boy," they says, "just look what America done to you! When you left, you was of a solitary and delicate disposition! Now look at you! Ragged and torn, you are! Ragged and torn!" "Aye," he said. "The Yanks they done it. And the bloody English!" And he raised his glass of whiskey even higher. And everyone raised theirs, too!

PEIG. It was a party. They didn't mean harm.

MAIRE. He didn't stay but half a year and he was back.

PEIG. But the letters. They weren't from Paddy Feeney.

MAIRE. I've got my own letters.

PEIG. What do you mean? What letters? What letters are you talking about? *(MAIRE pulls several letters from her apron pocket.)*

MAIRE. These letters. They're from Nellie.

PEIG. Nellie?

MAIRE. Nellie. Yes. Nellie.

PEIG. I didn't know she could write. I mean, I didn't think she *would* write.

MAIRE. For a year I've been saving these. She has a position with a family in Whitehall, New York. They have three children and two fine houses. Nellie says it takes one person just to tend to the silver and china. She says she's never done so much polishing!

PEIG. Her mother expects her back. She's always saying so.

MAIRE. Nellie won't be back.

PEIG. How do you know?

MAIRE. She's arranged to have me come work with her.

PEIG. Service? Oh, no, Maire, not service! It may be good enough for Nellie, but not you! You're not so common as her!

MAIRE *(reading)*. "Dear Maire: I dreamed last night I was in my father's house and there was a huge party about me. The whole town was there. It was so happy and gay with music and laughter. When I awoke, all I could think of was my family, my home ... "

PEIG *(interrupting)*. See there! She wants to come back! She can't bear being away!

MAIRE *(continuing).* "So I went to my window and looked out. What can I tell you? The trees and flowers greeted me like friends and I no longer felt sad. The more I am here, the more home seems like a dream." Seems to me she's bearing it quite well, Peig. *(Continuing.)* "The family I am living with—soon *your* family— is a very nice one. They're not Catholic but they are very kind. They have such refined manners! You should like them very much. Every Sunday the other girl and me we go to a splendid church, St. Stephen's. There they have *three* priests! *Three!* And incense and bells! Mass is very grand indeed! I'm so sorry about the penance Father Dugan gave to you. You must come at once, Maire. Here trespasses are forgiven more easily. Love, Nellie." And there's more: "The other girl and I bought new hats that are so very fine. We turn heads on our strolls. Everyone says so!" She's happy, Peig. All her letters are like this. Every one. *(She puts the letters away.)*

PEIG. She always was one for exaggerating.

MAIRE. People around here don't talk like Nellie. It's always the sufferin', always the troubles. It never changes. Like these stones. *(She picks some up.)* They were here last year and the year before that and the year before that. Hundreds and hundreds of years these stones been here. And they don't change, Peig. They don't move. The water runs over them and out to sea, but they don't do anything. They sit! They just sit!

PEIG. But service! Maire, you can't...!

MAIRE. Why can't I? Look at me. I've worn this apron all my life. I don't remember ever putting it on. It's just been a part of me like my hand or my leg.

PEIG. It's what we are, Maire.

MAIRE. It's what we *been*. And what has it meant? What have we carried in these deep pockets? That we can cook and clean and serve our fathers and our older brothers till "World without an end, Amen"? That we can marry and serve our husbands? That we can starve like our mother and have too many children? No. I've carried these things and I won't carry them no more. There isn't a man in the county I'd have, anyway. Either daft, drunk, or stupid, they are. They're all stones, just stones.

PEIG. Is that what you see for us?

MAIRE. I carry letters now. They tell me I can wear a new hat and take a stroll on a bright, sunny Sunday.

PEIG. Is that what you see?

MAIRE. They tell me I can be changed ... transformed. Nellie was a simple village girl a few months ago. Now she turns heads in Whitehall, New York.

PEIG. And do you believe she still is ... simple? *(They both laugh.)* Will you write to me, then, Maire, the way Nellie wrote to you?

MAIRE. I'll send you bundles of letters. You'll have to sew another pocket into your apron! *(MAIRE walks to the edge of the water and drops all the stones but one. PEIG joins her.)*

PEIG. Who will walk with me along the strand? Who will talk with me and share secrets? Stones. Yes, look at all the stones. This land is covered with them. Remember how we collected them when we were silly young girls? Just the two of us, we were. So silly, weren't we? We'd collect them in our apron pockets. You'd save yours up.

So many stones you had. You'd polish them and name them after all the girls at school you didn't like.

MAIRE. And boys!

PEIG. And boys. Then you'd toss them into the water. You'd fling them as far as you could way out over the waves. "There!" you'd say. "Let that be the end to you!"

MAIRE. Maire McKenna and her little toad of a brother, Liam. I threw in many stones for them! Margaret Dunn ... Jamie Donnelly ...

PEIG. You said you'd send them all to a watery grave. I thought for sure you'd be struck dead by lightning for talkin' so!

MAIRE. Boys and girls. Aunts and uncles. Priests and nuns. I had a lot more stones in my apron pocket than you knew!

PEIG. Priests and nuns?! Tell me you didn't throw priests and nuns into the ocean!

MAIRE. I took pleasure in it.

PEIG *(crossing herself)*. Oh, no!

MAIRE. For every slap on the hand, every cuff to the ear. Father Dugan was always passing out the penances like they was candy at Christmas, don't you know?! "A little extra 'Our Father.' Just one more. Or maybe another! That'll teach you, my girl! That'll hold you for another week!" *(She changes her voice to higher pitch.)* "Hold out your hand, Maire McMahon. Hold it up high. That's it. Now take what the good Lord wants you to have! Jesus, Mary, and Joseph know this hurts me more than it hurts you!" Snap with the ruler! Snap! I saved up so many stones, Peig. I had to rid myself of them. No girl's pockets could be that deep! Here, throw one in. *(She picks up a stone and hands it to PEIG.)*

PEIG. Priests and nuns! *(She crosses herself.)* It would kill our mother and father if they knew.

MAIRE. Go ahead, toss it!

PEIG. I can't.

MAIRE. You've got an arm, haven't you? Toss it!

PEIG. Who is it?

MAIRE. Who is it?

PEIG. Yes, who is it?

MAIRE. Why, anyone. Anyone at all. Some poor soul makes life a misery.

PEIG. I don't know... I—I can't... No, I can't! *(She drops the stone. MAIRE picks it up.)*

MAIRE. It's just a stone! It's useless, Peig! Look at it! Useless! It'll weigh you down!

PEIG. You throw it. I'll watch you.

MAIRE. All right. Who'll it be, then? *(They pause, thinking, then...)*

MAIRE & PEIG *(in unison)*. Paddy Feeney! *(Both laugh with surprise. MAIRE feels the rock with her hand.)*

PEIG. Ragged and torn, he is.

MAIRE. Of a solitary and delicate disposition.

PEIG. A shadow of his former self.

MAIRE & PEIG *(in unison)*. Poor, poor boy. *(MAIRE throws the stone. They both watch its trajectory as it hits the water way out in the dark. Then MAIRE picks up other stones and throws them wildly and excitedly till she is out of breath.)*

MAIRE. There! It's finished!

PEIG. Finished?

MAIRE. All the stones I been throwing these long years... With every one I was making a path across that water. I could see it stretched out before me, straight and shining, so beautiful. Like a vision, it was. Just beneath the waves. It'll hold me up, that path made of stones. I'll walk across it all the way to America, I will!

PEIG. A path?

MAIRE. All the way to America! Tonight when they were playing the pipes and singing so sad for me, all I could think was how I was going to walk...no, *dance* on those stones—those dead, lifeless, godforsaken stones.

PEIG. Will you send me letters?

MAIRE. You already asked me that.

PEIG. Tell me again.

MAIRE. Until you believe what I say.

PEIG. I'll carry them in my apron pocket.

MAIRE. And you'll read them over and over again.

PEIG. It's such a long way.

MAIRE. Not very. (*MAIRE picks up a stone and hands it to PEIG. PEIG looks at the stone for a moment, then at MAIRE. She steps forward with the stone in her hand as the lights dim to black.*)

END

ROWING TO AMERICA
by Kitty Chen

<u>CHARACTERS</u>:

GIRL, about 12, bright and inquiring, an enchanting, playful quality; she is special

SISTER, about 17, serious countenance interrupted by an astonishingly beautiful smile; more mature and responsible than her years

Notes

Although younger actors would be ideal, both characters may be played by older actors who have an intrinsic youthfulness. They should be Asian, African, or Latino, *but the two should not be the same race*. They must be comfortable with the lyrical, non-naturalistic speech and physical style.

A heavy, dramatic interpretation should be avoided, as should any temptation to ennoble, politicize, or "victimize" these characters and their situation. They are women in a tough situation, who have the imaginative power to see their way out.

The tone is lyrical and poetic. There is a magical, playful quality about this world. Simplicity and clarity should be the guiding principle.

SCENE ONE

AT RISE: *The sky is midnight blue, with a crescent moon and a few stars, the sound of waves slapping the side of a boat. GIRL sits on a simple box or bench, rowing with oars. All other objects may be mimed or suggested. SISTER is in shadow.*

GIRL. I'm rowing to America. The only thing I brought with me is a picture of a smile. Here in my head. Strong and radiant like the sun. The smile of my sister. "When we grow up and go to America, everything will be all right," she would say to me. She told me all sorts of things about America. Have you heard them too? She said the streets are paved with gold lamé. A dollar a day keeps the doctor away. Apple pie and huckleberry finn for breakfast. Milk and honey flow down the avenue Fifth Avenue. A chicken in every pot-pie. Where the sun never stops shining, and spacious skies are blue, and amber grains are always waving at you... When we get there, we will wave back. Look, sister—they've come to greet us! Hello! We're here—we've come to America—

(Lights come up on SISTER, who is waving GIRL away.)

SISTER. Forgive me, dear sister. You'll understand when you're older. Now, row! And sing! For me!
GIRL. Don't leave me! *(Lights fade on SISTER. GIRL watches until she disappears from sight.)* All right all right! I'll row—I'll sing! *(Sings.)*

"Row row row your boat, gently down the stream,

Merrily, merrily, merrily, merrily, life is but a
     dream ..:
Row row row your boat, gently down the stream,
Merrily, merrily, merrily, merrily, life is but a
     dream ... "

I'm tired. I don't know how far America is. Maybe I'll
wash up. "You must always look your best," sister said.
What if I should suddenly run into America without
warning?

(SISTER appears and combs GIRL's hair.)

GIRL. I catch the rainwater to drink and wash my face and
my hands. I've learned to be like a cat. It's important to
stay clean and neat. She would comb and braid my hair
with her strong, quick hands. Two neat, fat braids, like
sausage twins. She never pinched or pulled, the way
Mother did.

*(Lights brighten. GIRL breaks away from SISTER,
laughing. They are younger.)*

SISTER. Hah! Now I've got you! If you don't sit still, I'm
going to pinch and pull your hair so hard you will long
for Mother to pinch and pull!
GIRL. You would never hurt me.
SISTER. No. I would never ever hurt you. *(Gives her a
sudden pinch!)*
GIRL. You're smiling! I made you smile! Why don't you
smile all the time? Like you used to.

SISTER. I'm not as I used to be. Soon I will no longer be young. When a girl is no longer young, they take away ... *(She pauses.)*

GIRL. What do they take away? You look so sad.

SISTER. When you're older you'll know. Now sing my favorite song! About the little fisherman.

GIRL. Only if you smile. I want to count your teeth! How I wish I had your shining teeth. Like a string of the finest pearls. *(SISTER smiles)* Will you pinch and pull my hair when we go to America?

SISTER. Of course. When we grow up and go to America, everything will be all right. Now warm my heart, dear sister. But softly, for safety's sake.

GIRL *(sings)*.

"Wynken, Blynken, and Nod one night
Sailed off in a wooden shoe,
Sailed on a river of crystal light
Into a sea of dew.
'Where are you going, and what do you wish?'
The old moon asked the three.
'We have come to fish for the herring fish
That live in this beautiful sea;
Nets of silver and gold have we!'
Said Wynken, Blynken and Nod."

(Lights change back. SISTER recedes into shadow.)

GIRL. Where is your smile now, dear sister? Does it still hurt?

SISTER. Row.

GIRL. I better row. "Row row row your boat/ gently down the stream/ merrily merrily merrily ..." *(Etc. She sees something float by.)* Oh. Another piece of paper! *(She mimes fishing a magazine out of the water. Reads.)* "Among the universe of component CD players, it seems senseless to buy a single-play model for $100 when it's possible to buy a changer for as little as $125. The "*universe* of component CD players." What does C-D stand for? *(Searches page.)* The D is for disk. The C is for ... cosmic? What else could it be? A *universe* of *cosmic* disks. *(Sings.)*

> "Hello, Moon
> Good night, Moon
> I row by your light
> I sleep in your arms
> I sing to your charms
> A cosmic disk in the sky.
> A thrill of hope
> A glow of hope
> I keep on rowing
> But why am I going?
> Hello, Moon
> Good night, Moon
> Good night, Moon. Good night."

SISTER. "Such a lovely voice," they always said. "Better not to sing too much."

SCENE TWO

(Girl catches a fish)

GIRL. Come on, little fish. What's the use of fighting? I'm famished! Aha! Now I shall wrap you in seaweed, and what a tasty sandwich! *(She watches the fish thrash in the moonlight.)* Pearly little fish. How can I eat you? *(Starts to throw it back.)*

SISTER. Eat!—or you will not live to see America.

GIRL. I have to eat you. Forgive me! *(She proceeds to eat it. She sees another magazine float by.)* More paper! "Tests show how you can eat real eggs again. Egg World's eggs are better than other eggs." WHAT DOES THAT MEAN?!! Why can't people in America eat real eggs? What are real eggs? Why are Egg World's eggs better than other eggs? Why do they need tests to show how to eat an egg?

SISTER. Always so many questions! You must row! *(GIRL, annoyed by ad, turns the page.)*

GIRL. "Lascivious Lucy lurks in every lustful heart. Call 1-9-0-0 L-U-S T-F-U-L." *(Horror turns to curiosity. She examines Lucy's face.)* Her smile. It's so false! It makes her ugly!

SISTER. It's a custom in many countries, when a young girl is no longer young...they take away her crowning glory, her greatest gift...

GIRL. IT HAS NO STRENGTH.

SISTER. They take away her STRENGTH. That way people will love you more and fear you less.

GIRL. But here she is for the world to see!

SISTER. One or two modest gifts in a girl is safe. But to shine like a star, is to arouse Fear. Envy. Lust... And disrupt the harmony.

GIRL. Why? We should have *more love!* More harmony!

SISTER. Some time, some place, it may be so.

GIRL. HOW do they take them away?

SISTER. There are many different ways.

(SISTER begins to fade into shadow. GIRL sits quietly staring, as if at her past and future. Sounds of wind and rough seas grow. She starts up as if from a dream.)

GIRL. WHERE ARE YOU TAKING HER? Then I heard my mother's voice. "Go to sleep, we're taking a walk." I am not a child! We don't take walks in the middle of the night. *(Looking out window.)* My sister, my mother, and all the other mothers march across the moonlit field, like a procession of ravens... smaller and smaller. I wait by the window all night. Deep inside me, in a place that has no name, the sun begins to die.

(OPTIONAL: As she dozes fitfully, disturbing images, possibly slides or puppets, float across stage—young women of every race and color with shaved heads, no teeth, bound feet, taped mouths, shroud-covered, etc.)

(Morning. SISTER enters.)

GIRL. They're coming back. Why is that old woman wearing my sister's clothes, her body bowed in pain? She lifts her face to look at my mother. It's sister! Her mouth... HER MOUTH IS EMPTY! SHE HAS NO TEETH!

(Lights change. GIRL bangs on a door.)

GIRL. Please let me see her. I won't disturb her rest. I WANT TO SEE HER! I hate you, Mother! How could you do that to her—your own daughter? *(Pause.) Your* mother...? When *you* were no longer young? *(She begins sadly to understand.)*

(Lights change. SISTER enters.)

SISTER. They gave me false teeth, cast from a mold of Little Brother's mouth. Am I ugly and gray?

GIRL *(touches her mouth).* No, my precious sun. Does it still hurt?

SISTER *(nods).* Harmony is preserved, the people are safe.

GIRL. I hate the people! Their harmony is wrong!

SISTER. Hush. Come quickly.

GIRL *(as they run to the boat).* America?

SISTER. Yes. Goodbye, dear sister. *(Hugs GIRL fiercely for a long time.)*

GIRL. Wait! No!

SISTER. GO! Do as I say!

GIRL. No! Not without you!

SISTER. It's too late for me. You're still young and whole. I want you to sing and shine like a star. Please go.

GIRL. I won't go without you!

SISTER. Do you want them to slit your throat? Etch tiny marks over your larynx? Make it a knot of scar tissue— strangle your voice forever? Now go! *(GIRL starts to cry. SISTER leads her to boat and pushes off. They stand in same postures and relationship as in first scene.)* Forgive me, dear sister. You'll understand when you're older. Now row! And sing! For me!

GIRL. Don't leave me! *(SISTER fades from sight.)* I'm rowing to America. Where the streets are paved with gold lamé, and I can shine like a star. But deep inside, the sun is frozen black. *(Something floats by.)* Another American shopping paper. Every day, more and more. *(She stares at a picture.)* It's her smile! They have her smile in America! *(Reads.)* "Smile whenever you like! Never feel self-conscious about less than perfect teeth. Get laminated!" I'll get her smile back for her—I'll take it back to her! I'll sing, and row to America. For her. *(Sings.)*

"Smile, smile, whenever you like.

In America everybody smiles.

It is good if you smile.

If you smile, you are good."

(Lights of city skyline appear, and grow bigger and brighter.)

Look, sister. Look at all the lights. Shining like your smile. You haven't left me. I see your smile everywhere. It's here in my head, and my heart.

SISTER. Goodbye, little sister. Please forgive me. *(Exits.)*

GIRL. They've come to greet us! Hello!—We're here! We've come to America!... Now everything will be all right.

END

SLAVE COFFLE W/ OBSERVER
by J. Rufus Caleb

CHARACTERS:

CLARA, enslaved African-American
CHARLES, enslaved African-American
OBSERVER, European-American, either female or male

The pre-recorded voices of the INTERVIEWER and
BALL are African-American.

TIME: Some transcendent place.

SETTING: *The stage is bare and lit with a light that suggests dusk. The sounds of a reel-to-reel tape recorder is heard being turned on and cueing.*

AT RISE: *CLARA and CHARLES enter and take positions downstage. The OBSERVER enters and takes a position slightly upstage and to the side of CLARA and CHARLES. A sound bed of a farm is heard: wood chopping, a dog barking, a car driving by, a door opening/closing, running and giggling children—all rising in volume. Suddenly, the voice of the INTERVIEWER is heard.*

INTERVIEWER. Testing, testing, testing ...

BALL. Mister, you jes' shoo tha' dog 'way. Y'all chillens gwan somewheres. Gwan, git.

INTERVIEWER. Testing. I think we're ready. WORKS PROGRESS ADMINISTRATION, tape number forty-three. Interview with Mr. Charles Ball. July 28, 1938. Our location is the Ball farm, Dorchester County, South Carolina.

BALL. Git yo' noses off tha' machine.

INTERVIEWER. I don't mind them, Mr. Ball. You kids be quiet. *(Pause.)* Mr. Ball reckons his age to be eighty-two.

BALL. Eighty-four, sir. Eighty-four. Now what you want me to do?

INTERVIEWER. Oh, just talk about your life.

BALL. Don't know's the Lord go' give me 'nough time to tell my whole life.

INTERVIEWER. Tell me what you remember.

BALL. Well, suh, I can 'member a way back.

INTERVIEWER *(pause)*. You must have known slavery.

BALL. Knowed it some—much as a young pup go' know.

INTERVIEWER. I'm anxious—Mr. Ball, I'm anxious to know 'bout that time. *(Pause.)* What do you remember?

BALL. Heap o' things. Tha' car what jes' druve by? 'Member when Mr. James bought it. 'Member when ever' las' one these chillens born. They mamas and daddas, too.

INTERVIEWER. Slavery, Mr. Ball. Anything?

BALL. Aw, tha' stuff do' 'long to me.

INTERVIEWER. Whatchu mean?

BALL. 'Long to my grandda.

INTERVIEWER. Your grandda?

BALL. Was tol' to me.

INTERVIEWER *(coaxing)*. What he tell you—'bout slavery?

BALL. Heap o' things.

INTERVIEWER *(pause)*. Like what?

BALL *(pause)*. I know how us come here.

INTERVIEWER *(quickly)*. To America?

BALL. To Souse Car'lina. Right here to Dorchester County.

INTERVIEWER. From where?

BALL. Dunno.

INTERVIEWER. You don't know?

BALL. Guess, do' none us know. *(Deep, steady breathing. The whirl of the machine reels.)*

INTERVIEWER. Mr. Ball? Sir?

(The lights rise on the stage. When CLARA, CHARLES and the OBSERVER speak, they are perfectly still.)

CLARA. Was near sundown when the driver come to the tobaccy barn with the piece o' paper in his hand. I was front the barn, jes' done stringing the last bunch of them green tobaccy leaves to the last stick I was gonna do that day. Waiting for one o' the mens to take it in the barn for hanging. Nothing more I had to do that night, 'cept throw some water on my patch o' plants. Take my bowl for even' rations. Stand in the yard, lissen to ove'seer Bill call off names o' ones to draw punishment for this that t'other. I was dead tired and the baby I was carrying lay like a stone in my stomach. Us that was standing outside the tobaccy barn, we knew each other, don' nobody know *his* face. Driverman lookin' 'round, don't know who is who. "Clara!" Driverman yell out my name from the paper. Gwan stand by the pecan tree. Driverman called Aunt Cora boy to come from out the barn, to stand by the pecan tree. Driverman see the Ibo-man what got cuts on his face. Nod him down the ladder from the eaves of the barn, to stand by the pecan tree. Time he took to call us three names, the sun ain't moved. I'm looking right at it. Sun ain' move, I was thinking. Driverman wave his paper to us three to walk direct towards the sun. When we walking for even' meal, the sun is over my left shoulder, an' near swallowed by the trees. Ain' near time for walking.

CHARLES. The women was just tied together with a rope 'bout the size of a bed cord, like a halter 'round the neck of each. Were nineteen women. Clara was third to be tied. But the men were chained. A strong iron collar was fit close around each of our necks, and padlocked. A chain of iron was passed through the loop of each padlock, except for the first and last links. The chain run for near one hundred feet, the blacksmith said, and end with the Ibo-man. I was the stoutest and strongest, and the chain began at my neck. I was the first of thirty-two men. I counted the men behind me by the start and stop of the hammer blows, and judged their distance from how far behind me the blows came. The blacksmith used the same count for each man. The blacksmith was called Hodges. I asked him, "Hodges—what's this mean?" *(Pause.)* "Hodges—where they taking us?" *(Pause.)* Hodges was kneeling between me and a man I did not know. My arm was resting on the blacksmith's anvil. In this way he handcuffed us in pairs. With iron staples and bolts, the blacksmith worked his hammer on a short chain of a foot's length, uniting my left arm to the stranger's right arm. And the poor man to whom I was ironed wept like an infant when the heavy hammer fastened the bolts that kept the cuffs from slipping from our wrists. "Hodges—why double-chain us so?" He nudged us forward, then answered when the second pair reached his anvil: " 'Cause massa say so." *(Pause.)* The line of thirty-two moved forward, from single to pairs, as each man— *(CLARA screams.)* Clara had heard her husband—my nephew—cry out. Word whispered up to me, along the chain said: "The hammer slipped."

CLARA. Uncle Charles?

CHARLES. I could not answer her.

CLARA. Uncle Charles?

CHARLES. I could not bear to answer her.

CLARA. Uncle Charles!?

CHARLES. What!?

CLARA. I ain't go' survive this.

CHARLES. I had lived forty-eight years, had wife and children. Was I free to find a rope, I should have hanged myself. *(Pause.)* When the blacksmith finished, we stepped onto the road, into the traffic.

(A sound bed of modern highway noise, automobile horns. CHARLES and CLARA take positions upstage of the OBSERVER. The OBSERVER shading her eyes, watches them. The highway bed moves into the background.)

OBSERVER. The first line of Negroes came 'round the bend, along the path that parallels the road, chained at the neck, and shuffling their feet like in a dream. My fist let go my pail handle; the few pecans I had gathered clinked and rattled into the bottom of the pail. I moved from beneath the pecan tree, across the short field of grass, to the edge of the road opposite them. The second line of Negroes, tied at the neck with white cord, came 'round the bend. *(The highway bed rises sharply, moves into the background.)* I had dropped the pail when traffic burst over the road between them and me. *(Pause.)* I saw the lines had stopped. Thirty-two men. Nineteen women. My companions had not noticed us. I called to my cousin. I asked, How do they eat? Oh, the driver provides. He put my pail back into my hand, smoothed my fingers closed. From whence have they come? North of us. And are heading? South. The Carolinas, Mississippi. Even the Louisiana Territory. *(Pause.)* My companions could tell me nothing but that such a possession as I was observing is called a "coffle." And one certain thing more: Where these Negroes come from, they are no longer needed, or can no longer be afforded. *(Pause.)* He lifted his pail, to remind me of the purpose of our afternoon's mission. *(Pause.)* The Negroes stood utterly spent, without animation. The Negroes stood against the green sweep of grass and tall trees, dark thin sticks in fragments of clothing. The Negroes stood, waiting. And then a woman passed a tiny thing to the first man in line. Onto his unchained arm she nestled—a baby—feet and arms draped his wrist, like an open cuff. Then she pointed her arm to me, and her husband followed her gaze. And the Negroes moved off. I turned away, when the traffic burst between us.

(CLARA, CHARLES and the OBSERVER exit. The lights shift to suggest dusk. The farm sound bed rises. The whirl of tape recorder reels.)

INTERVIEWER. Mr. Ball? Is there anything more about the African, Mr. Ball? Where was the Ibo-man sold?

BALL *(pause)*. Grandda say once that somewhere 'long the way, Li'l Clara point out a fat pecan tree what was dripping with nuts. *(Whirl of tape reels.)*

END

HOMELAND
by Sachi Oyama

CHARACTERS:

KEIKO, Asian female
STOREKEEPER
NEIGHBOR LOMELI
HIGH-TECH NEIGHBOR

SETTING: *A bare stage with mutable sets which transform from a neighborhood to a home to a classroom by suggestion of chairs, boxes.*

AT RISE: *A neighborhood.*

NEIGHBOR LOMELI. Yoooooooooooooo, Keiko. Ohhhhh, there you go again. Carrying your little one. You people spoil your kids.

KEIKO. Hello, Mi ... se ... suu ... uh ...

NEIGHBOR LOMELI. ... spoil your men. Carrying their jackets to the car and all. This is America. You gotta do like us Americans, for Chrissake.

KEIKO. M ... se ... suu ... uh ... Ro ... Ro ... me ... ri?

NEIGHBOR LOMELI. Lomeli.

KEIKO. We came to America to start a new life. My husband, Ryuichi, said there was much opportunity here. He would become a sushi chef and someday own his own

47

restaurant. I would escape the memories of my first marriage. My husband said I should not speak Japanese or I would never learn English. The Americans will make fun of us, call us F.O.B.s. Ryuichi told me that meant "Fresh off the Boat." We came by plane. So I spoke my language at home with my husband. And two nights a week I went to ESL, English as a Second Language.

(A school bell. A classroom.)

I brush my teeth.
I comb my hair.
How do you do, Mrs. Rodriguez?

OTHER STUDENTS *(mumbling)*. How do you do, Mrs. Rodriguez?

KEIKO. Do you think it will rain today?

OTHER STUDENTS *(mumbling)*. Do you think it will rain today?

KEIKO. Do you think it will hail today?

OTHER STUDENTS *(mumbling)*. Do you think it will hail today?

KEIKO. Do you think it will snow today?

OTHER STUDENTS *(mumbling)*. Do you think it will snow today?

KEIKO. Why do they have these sentences in Los Angeles? In Los Angeles, there is only one weather. Ryuichi was right. It was far better to be away from people that spoke my language. I learned quickly. I learned well. I did not want to fail again.

I am feeling happy today, Mrs. Rodriguez. *(Beat.)*
I am feeling sad today, Mrs. Rodriguez. *(Beat.)*
I am feeling lonely today, Mrs. Rodriguez.

I cheated. I watched Japanese television so I could hear my language from someone other than Ryuichi. I watched it too much and began to feel guilty. So at night, before my husband came home, I watched American television. I liked *Mama's Family.* I did not understand what they said. But I knew it was funny. My favorite program was *A Team* on channel 11. I could understand everything, no one dies, and everyone speaks simple English. In the morning I watched *Sesame Street.* That was when the first child came. A son. And later a daughter.

STOREKEEPER. You know, Keiko, I think you should leave your kids with a sitter once in a while. You don't even come here to the store without them. How do you expect to enjoy life. Isn't that what you came to America for? $10.56.

KEIKO. Thank you ... Mr. ... Mr. ... uh ...

STOREKEEPER. Call me Ben. Do you have a penny?

KEIKO. I was happy. America was my home. My children were Americans. They were like myself, breathing the air of another country yet not rooted to it. I was alone— with my children, my husband. I needed nothing else. They made up my world.

(Koto in background.)

It was always the sound of the koto perhaps, or the smell of the ocean that reminded me. I could understand the sights and sounds so clearly, with no effort, no strain. With English there was always so much effort.

HIGH-TECH NEIGHBOR. Lesson Number One, use the dryer. It doesn't ruin the children's clothes to be spun in the dry cycle. You have to learn to be high-tech.

KEIKO. Uhmm... Do you think... uh... it will...

HIGH-TECH NEIGHBOR. I thought you people... you know... Your country makes all the VCRs.

KEIKO. ...uh...rain...today?

HIGH-TECH NEIGHBOR. Look at you now. A perfectly healthy woman with a perfectly healthy husband and all you do is take care of him and the kids. That's not what family life is in America. Get a Maytag. They're the best.

NEIGHBOR LOMELI. You enjoy yourself. And *while* you have the kids you enjoy yourself. Go to Mexico. Have a burrito without the kids taking half of it.

ALL. You know what I mean.

STOREKEEPER. $12.18. Do you have anything smaller?

KEIKO. Maybe it will...uh...snow?

NEIGHBOR LOMELI. Snow? What are you talking about? Listen up, honey, this country ain't for men and kids like your country. We don't kiss nobody's feet. I just wanted to tell you the way it is. You seem like a nice gal. Take some lessons here from a natural American. Oh...Oh... and thanks for them little rice crackers.

(Koto.)

KEIKO. I am among strangers. Strangers who do not know that the smell of ocean water takes me back to my homeland. It is the same ocean, the same water, and yet it is different. The shores are the same and yet different. They do not hear the same songs as I and weep. It is always the first sights, the first sounds, the first smells.

(School bell.)

How do you do, Mrs. Rodriguez?
I hope you are fine today.
I hope you will be fine tomorrow.
I hope you will be fine the day after tomorrow.

END

FAMOUS ALI
by Robert Clyman

CHARACTERS:

ALI, an Afghanistani seeking American citizenship
HARRIS, a Unites States Immigration interviewer
LATOYA, a young Haitian woman with American
    citizenship

SETTING: *An interview room at the Bureau of Immigration and Naturalization.*

AT RISE: *HARRIS is questioning ALI, an applicant for citizenship. LATOYA sits next to ALI.*

HARRIS. Dubcek, for instance.
ALI. Yes.
HARRIS. Great man. A hero.
ALI. Truly.
HARRIS. The way he stood against the tanks.
ALI. Actually, he was Czechoslovakia. I am Afghanistan.
HARRIS *(slight beat)*. I was speaking in general.
ALI. In that case, truly. Dubcek.
HARRIS. Of course, you're from Afghanistan. Land of the mujhadin.
ALI. That is us.
HARRIS. Great men. Heroes.

53

ALI. You make Ali blush.

HARRIS. We were much too slow to respond. To the atrocities. I've always said that.

ALI. Ali is not angry. I am just happy to kiss your earth.

HARRIS. A difficult time, I imagine? I mean, the war.

ALI. Much suffering. My wife, Elena?

HARRIS. Yes?

ALI. Shot.

HARRIS. I'm sorry.

ALI. Like a dog.

HARRIS. How awful.

ALI. One bullet to the back of the head. I almost go mad.

HARRIS. Naturally.

ALI. Threw down my rifle. Ran into... how do you call it... everywhere chaos...

HARRIS. The fray?

ALI. Yes. Hail of bullets everywhere.

HARRIS. Unbelievable.

ALI. It is how things were there. In time, the pain is less. Always Ali dreams of the future. But what kind of future will it be? Then the chance to begin again... to have a life in America.

HARRIS *(flipping through the file)*. I'm sorry, did you say "shot"?

ALI. Yes, one bullet to the back of the head.

HARRIS. Because it says here your wife is still alive in Kabul.

ALI *(beat)*. Says that?

HARRIS. Now that I'm looking, I also see you were assigned to inventory during the war. Processing the arrival of dry goods.

ALI. Important work. Received many thanks.

HARRIS. I'm sure. I just wonder how you encountered a hail of bullets while you were working indoors.

ALI *(slight beat)*. Ran outside.

HARRIS. But you were in Kabul...nowhere near the front.

ALI *(slight beat)*. Ran for miles.

HARRIS. Do you see where I'm pointing? The only reason it mentions your wife is that she's been trying to find you. She claims you disappeared without leaving a note.

ALI *(after looking shiftily for several beats, suddenly brightens)*. Thank God, Elena lives!

HARRIS *(somewhat suspiciously)*. Yes, apparently.

ALI. How she escapes is a miracle.

HARRIS. She can be reached through the embassy.

ALI. We live in great times.

HARRIS. I imagine you'll be wanting to get back as soon as possible.

ALI *(slight beat)*. Return to Kabul?

HARRIS. Yes, that's where she is.

ALI *(beat)*. No...too late.

HARRIS. How's that?

ALI. After grief, tore love for Elena out of my heart. Found joy again in the arms of Latoya. *(LATOYA smiles at HARRIS.)*

HARRIS *(to LATOYA)*. And you're from...?

ALI. Haiti.

HARRIS *(to LATOYA)*. Exactly where in Haiti...?

ALI. Port-au-Prince. We find many things in common. So much suffering. When I meet Latoya, she hardly speaks.

HARRIS. It seems to me she still hardly speaks.

ALI. Very shy. Lot going on below surface. She is my little honey bun.

HARRIS. I see.

ALI. Gonna be a fabulous wedding. Plenty of toot and whistles.

HARRIS. Exactly how long have you known her?

ALI. Three days. Almost four.

HARRIS. And this doesn't strike you as rushing things?

ALI. Know right away when I meet her. Head over heels for my honey bun.

HARRIS. Where did you meet?

ALI. Little coffee shop. Meeting arranged by my cousin.

HARRIS. Interesting word... "arranged."

ALI. Sorry, my English...I am not meaning "arranged"?

HARRIS. That's what I need to find out. *(Beat.)* Latoya, how did you first meet Mr. Rashid's cousin? *(LATOYA just smiles at him.)* Did either Mr. Rashid or his cousin offer you any money to come here today? *(She continues to smile.)*

ALI. I think she likes you. She is giving you Latoya's most happy smile.

HARRIS *(to ALI)*. Do you see the problem I'm having? Your soul mate doesn't seem to speak any English.

ALI. Still, Latoya a definite fox, don't you think?

HARRIS. Correct me if I'm wrong, but is your Haitian correspondingly weak?

ALI. That is so. But is it also not so that a man and a woman can never really...what is the word...communicate?

HARRIS. Maybe not perfectly, although a couple of words in common are generally thought to help. *(Slight beat.)* Mr. Rashid, allow me to voice my suspicion. Latoya is not your little honey bun but, rather, a woman whom you or your cousin paid to enter into a strictly fiduciary arrangement with you, so that you could defraud the

United States government in your bogus attempt to seek
American citizenship.

ALI *(beat, then turning to LATOYA)*. Sweetie pie, tell the
mister about that we are in love.

LATOYA *(wooden, clearly scripted, to ALI)*. You my one
and only. From day I was born, was never no one like
you. Ali a dream come true. Wish to bear you many
children and live in white picket fence. If anyone not
believe me, they are racist and lose big in court.

ALI *(beat, then confidently to HARRIS)*. Apologize to
honey bun.

HARRIS. I have never heard a less credible story. This
woman clearly hasn't the slightest interest in you.

ALI *(beat)*. All right, relationship is for now a little bit on
the rocks.

HARRIS. Watch this. *(To LATOYA, slowly.)* Latoya, I
would like you to marry me instead of Ali. I'm willing
to pay you more than he is... *(Taking out his wallet.)*
...One thousand dollars.

LATOYA *(beat)*. This be cash dollars?

HARRIS. Yes.

LATOYA *(beat, then leaning forward to HARRIS)*. You
my one and only. From day I was born, was never no
one...

HARRIS *(cutting her off)*. Yes, that's enough, young lady.
(Beat, to ALI.) Well?

ALI *(after several beats)*. All right, you see through Ali.
Truth is, I pay her three hundred dollars and buy her
later today ham and cheese sandwich.

HARRIS. I thought it was something like that. *(Writing.)*
Please take this form to Room 204 down the hall.

ALI. You turn Ali down?

HARRIS. I'm afraid so.

ALI. How about fact that I am desperate political refugee?

HARRIS. The war is over. How can you be a political refugee?

ALI. Please understand. From little boy, I love only to bake. Cookies of every kind. Pass down from grandmother. But Ali come up with own secret ingredient. No matter, you can try to strangle me with lamp cord, you will not find out what it is.

HARRIS. I really don't see ...

ALI. I visit cousin here a year ago from Christmas. He try my cookies. Says nothing tastes so good in the world. Wants now to have fancy shop where everyone eat my cookies. Soon we are all be rolling in dough.

HARRIS *(impatiently)*. Yes, but how were you being oppressed?

ALI. Cannot sell cookies in Afghanistan.

HARRIS. But you can't really call that oppression.

ALI. Try to set up little stand near my home. Party chief in my village drive up in jeep and tell me cookies are decadent. Says it gives people idea that life is sweet when life is bitter struggle against forces of counter-revolution. I say just try one of my cookies ... especially hazelnut raisin. He says nothing ... just stares at me. Then he push over my stand. Hundreds of cookies. Nothing to do but feed them to sheep.

HARRIS. I can see why that upset you. But that doesn't change the fact that America has to have standards. You can't expect us to go to the mat because of your country's policy about sweets.

ALI. I am oppressed. Stuck in backward country where I cannot work.

HARRIS. Of course, you can work. You just can't sell cookies.

ALI. Selling cookies everything to me. Broke my heart to feed them to sheep.

HARRIS. Mr. Rashid, here's what I think. First you make up some sob story about a dead wife. On top of that, you bribe this woman into marrying you. Then, when I see through your obvious scam, you try to turn the fact that you bake into a political statement. You're what I would call an opportunist.

ALI *(beat)*. "Opportunist." Yes, this word I have heard. It means someone who wishes to take opportunity when there is none. You have opportunity to do whatever makes you happy, so no need to be opportunist. I try to be opportunist, so I can be like you.

HARRIS. I think you're twisting...

ALI. No, I am only with facts. My cousin says how are things in America. Have a wife... then one day have a different wife. Yes, I offer Latoya money. My cousin says a man in your country takes money to invest in the future. You tell me marriage to Latoya no good, so now I am political refugee. That is why your country is great. If one thing not work, a man can try something else. *(Beat.)* I read your newspaper. Everyone here complains. They live in greatest country in the world but say things are no good. I love your country. Why not if I stay, and they can go? Is it Ali's fault that I am not allowed to live here, because nobody in Afghanistan tries to kill me? Maybe your whole life nobody tries to kill you. Only difference is you were here first.

HARRIS *(after several beats)*. Do you know how many little shops there are here already that barely get by selling cookies? What makes you think you could even succeed?

ALI *(pointing to a cookie tin that LATOYA is holding)*. Latoya, show this man with the cookies. *(LATOYA opens the tin, removes a cookie and proceeds to chew it with languorous delight.)* No, give cookie to the mister. *(She offers the tin, and HARRIS selects one. He chews it, at first thoughtfully, then with evident pleasure.)* Even better with milk. *(LATOYA offers HARRIS a small carton of milk.)*

HARRIS. These are very good.

ALI. Take. Plenty of assortment for you and the missus.

HARRIS *(beat, as he eats and drinks)*. I suppose it is a form of oppression. Turning over your stand like that... we would never stand for it here.

ALI. Yes, this is such a good point. *(Beat.)* You could do it. One little scratch of the pencil. *(They stare at each other. Then HARRIS writes.)*

HARRIS. Take this to Room 203.

ALI. This is better than Room 204?

HARRIS *(beat)*. Welcome to America.

ALI. Thank you. *(Turning to LATOYA.)* Latoya, we are not to get married.

LATOYA *(beat)*. Ham and cheese sandwich, still?

ALI. No. Big dinner on Ali. *(ALI clutches the paper, grabs her hand and begins to rush off. Suddenly, he turns back.)*

HARRIS. Yes?

ALI. Ali has another idea. For very little dollars, nice immigration man could be Ali's silent partner. Soon can be rolling in dough.

HARRIS. I don't think so, but I appreciate the offer.

ALI. Nothing has to decide today. Always tomorrow in America. *(Lights fade.)*

END

For Joe Megel, a friend.

A MULE IN J.F.K.
by Keith Glover

CHARACTERS:

GUARD, African-American
RAMON, Latino, in his early 20s

SETTING: *The J.F.K. Airport detaining room.*

AT RISE: *Late night. A GUARD holds court behind a solitary desk. After a moment of boredom he rises and goes to check the door. (The coast is clear.) He locks the door. He returns to his throne behind the desk and takes out a bag of reefer and fires up a joint. He inhales, enjoying his late-night respite. He looks through a cloud of smoke at the only other thing in the room: a gurney. Resting on top of the gurney is a large black body bag. The GUARD takes another drag. (He scored some really good stuff.) He starts to flip through a New York Post newspaper which screams a heavily political headline as he continues to enjoy his weed. The body bag begins to unzip from the inside. From within comes RAMON ESTRELLA. Recently deceased.*

RAMON. Damn, it's cold in there. Mind if I come out for a while?
GUARD. Go ahead. Free country.

RAMON. Thank you. You are very kind.

GUARD. My fantasy, but first sign of trouble, back inside.

RAMON. I got you. *(Rest.)* I am in a lot of trouble, yes?

GUARD. Not anymore.

RAMON. Okay. At least you are honest. I like that? Make a mistake and you really pay the price, yes?

GUARD. You know it better than I.

RAMON. That is true. I should of come by boat. To hell with airplanes and airports. *(Rest.)* My English is okay, yes?

GUARD. I heard worse.

RAMON. I practiced a lot. At night, at day. I practice. I know when you come to this country you must speak the language. You don't speak the language you have trouble. My brothers told me that. So I took the hint and I learned.

GUARD. Yeah, you learned, but you didn't learn what you should of learned.

RAMON. Your English is good also.

GUARD. Should be.

RAMON. Yes. You took classes?

GUARD. Nope, but I got an advantage.

RAMON. What? Tell me.

GUARD. I was born here.

RAMON. Lucky break. Where?

GUARD. Bed-sty.

RAMON. That is far, no?

GUARD. Nope. Brooklyn.

RAMON. Brook-leen, I have heard of it.

GUARD *(moves to look at the world outside)*. But sometimes being from Brooklyn you feel like the land across the bridge is a shit-kicking world away, anyway.

RAMON. I don't understand.

GUARD. Don't expect you to. I was born here, raised here but man, a lot of times, I don't feel like it's my home. It should be, but I just wish I could leave. Yeah, man pack up and leave, the hell with this country.

RAMON. Not a nice thing to feel about your home.

GUARD. Nope, but tough tittie. It's how I feel.

RAMON. I always knew I would love it here. No matter how hard it is.

GUARD. That's 'cause you a fool.

RAMON. I am not a fool.

GUARD. No? Then what are you doing in that bag?

RAMON. A mistake in judgment.

GUARD. Yeah, well, so you say now. Listen to me, boss, I see what you don't see and I see it twenty-twenty. You bought into that American Dream fallacy. But that's okay. We all do. That's why we get here. My grandfather bought it. Came over from Haiti, proud as hell, and he caught hell from the moment he set foot on these damn shores till the day he died. Trying to prove to this country he was a man and kept being mistaken as a nigger. Last words on his lips was, "America is only good to make money. You can't live here like a man. Hell with it." Yep, those was his last words.

RAMON. That's not true for everyone.

GUARD. If you had made it here, hung around for a while, believe me, we would of seen eye to eye.

RAMON. No. This is the greatest country in the world. My brothers come here first and they told me to come quick. They told me of the things you have here if you work hard. They told me here a man could become rich in days! So I came.

GUARD. You got family here?

RAMON. Two brothers.

GUARD. What they doing? They making boo-coo money? If they are they must be pushing.

RAMON. Nah, they both work in restaurants as busboys. They are not for taking risks.

GUARD. That's your department, right?

RAMON. I wanted money fast. America you need money to enjoy it.

GUARD. You wanted to get rich in a day?

RAMON. Yes.

GUARD. Yeah, see you knew it was bullshit. You wanted to make some real money fast. Busing tables wasn't gonna get it, so you got into the mule program. Seen it before. I know. I only wish I could of told you that you was making a big mistake.

RAMON. A mistake for me, but still my family will be taken care of. It was worth it.

GUARD. You think so?

RAMON. Yes. The people I worked for will take care of me. They promised.

GUARD. Damn, you really are a believer in fairy tales. Even after what you done.

RAMON. No. The people I worked for will understand.

GUARD. I wouldn't count on it. They will probably be so pissed they might wipe out your whole family over what you did. A mule that doesn't do his part. A mule that doesn't deliver is bad news. An embarrassment.

RAMON. I did my part. Just seeing those dogs and all those men with badges made me nervous and that made my stomach turn.

GUARD. Yeah, made the stomach start flipping, made the acids boil in you scared little stomach, breaking the bags. Releasing that shit.

RAMON. Yes.

GUARD. And you are where you are.

RAMON. Yes.

GUARD. Tough break, but like I said, you should of known better.

RAMON. Listen, I always had a bad day. I don't need you to make me feel worse.

GUARD. Can't get no worse than how you feeling.

RAMON. You think you are better than me?

GUARD. No. Just smarter. I'm not spending the night at the body bag hotel. You is. You just want sympathy and you ain't gonna get it.

RAMON. I don't want it.

GUARD. Yes you do. You might even deserve a little but I ain't gonna give it to you. Nah, the hell with it. Listen, I'm tired of explaining things to people, when it don't make no difference in the axis of the axis, so get back in the bag.

RAMON. I will, just give me a moment. *(Rest.)*

GUARD. It's starting to hit you, right?

RAMON. Yes.

GUARD. That it's all over.

RAMON. Yes. I have made a mistake.

GUARD. Yep. Believed all the promises of America and let it put your life on the line. Wasn't worth it, was it?

RAMON. It would of been worth it. If I had won.

GUARD. I bet.

RAMON. I would of lived in style. I would of been somebody.

GUARD. You are somebody. You are a statistic. A stick
figure on the graph of American nightmares. The proud
dead owner of a busted gut full of heroin, who probably
leaves a mother and wife back home with nothing but
tears. Heartbroken, standing in mud from a outhouse toi-
let with your promises of a better life when you got back
still ringing in their ears. But they won't forget you.
They will place your picture back home against the wall
in the middle of candles and flowers, and people will
pass your portrait with sorrow in their eyes. Folks will
speak your name for years with a warning to others that
will fall on deaf ears. 'Cause somebody with a head fulla
dreams about America will be talked into doing the same
thing that you did. They will take their shot at being a
mule for rich folks, who send you jackasses up here like
the fools that you are, while they live back home in your
country like kings. They know where their paradise re-
sides. It's in the country you can't wait to leave, because
you bought into the lies that it is so damn better here.
Listen to me dead man, the folks who got you into this
mess, they don't believe in the American dream. They
know it's a con. That's why they stay at home. The
dream you dreaming is for suckers.

RAMON. You think you know it all?

GUARD. Man, I don't know nothing. But with guys like
you doing what you doing, I am learning all the time.

RAMON. I almost made it work. If I had walked a little
cooler. I'd been with a big car and a home with money
filling all my pockets.

GUARD. Man, get back in the bag. You are spoiling my
high. Look at me, I ain't got no high-school diploma. I
was born here. I got a G.E.D. Why you think you gonna

get here and jump in front of me in the line to a better life. If there was a way to make it I'd of found it already. I'm living and working for six bucks an hour here bored to tears every day. I can't wait till everybody leaves this tomb so I can get high and fantasize about a life outside of the one I am trapped in. And let me tell you, son, America is nowhere in it. America does not exist, except in the mind, and those with the ability to make it real are disinterested in making it so.

RAMON. Can I have a drag?

GUARD. Sure, this is America. At least I can be polite. *(RAMON takes a toke and starts to get back inside the bag.)* You ain't heard a word I said, have you?

RAMON. I have heard you.

GUARD. Would you do it again?

RAMON. To live America? To live for my dreams? Oh yes. We must have dreams even if we do not reach them. We have to try. *(RAMON gets back in the bag. Lights fade.)*

END

For Nancy Hou

LET US GO THEN
by Akhil Sharma

CHARACTERS:

ARJUN, an Indian man, early 50s
SWATI, an Indian woman, early 50s
VIJAY, an Indian man, early 20s

AT RISE: *Evening. ARJUN and SWATI sit on a sofa.*
SWATI is reading a paperback of T.S. Eliot poems. She
is softly reciting a poem to herself. She keeps pausing
and trying out various intonations. ARJUN sits with his
feet under him and wrapped in a shawl so that we can't
see his face. He is sleeping. On SWATI's side of the sofa
is a small clock. ARJUN burps. Beat. He burps again,
louder. The burp wakes him and he almost spills off the
sofa. ARJUN realizes what happened and chuckles.

ARJUN. What time is it?
SWATI. Five-ten. *(Trying out different voices.)*
    "Let us go then
    Let us go then
(She finds what she's looking for.)
    Let us go then, you and I
    When the evening is spread out against the sky
    Like a patient etherized upon a table."
(Her voice trembles.)

71

ARJUN *(deliberately interrupting).* I feel like I'm drugged. Some days I sleep more than I'm awake.

SWATI. "Let us go through certain half-deserted streets."

ARJUN. I don't know why you can't sleep. *(SWATI stops and glares at ARJUN, who burps a long one.)* That one burnt. Did Vijay come?

SWATI. If you walked around.

ARJUN. I'm sick. I know. I'm a doctor.

SWATI. You're a dentist. That's just better than a chiropractor.

ARJUN. Leave me alone. *(ARJUN can give it but can't take it. He is hurt and SWATI notes this and feels pity.)*

SWATI. I would but you're the only one in the house.

ARJUN. Do you have it memorized? I do from your readings. *(Recites with ridicule, a finger up in the air.)*
    "No! I am not Prince Hamlet, nor was meant to be;
    Am an attendant lord, one that will do
    To swell a progress, start a scene or two,"
    Boohoo; boohoo
    "Advise the prince; no doubt, an easy tool."

SWATI. I am going to read Hamlet.

ARJUN. Everything is a game to you. *(Pause.)* You know how difficult Hamlet is to read?

SWATI. I have my whole life. *(Beginning to feel her kindness break down.)*

ARJUN *(bitterly).* You have your whole life. I have my whole life. Everything is a game.

SWATI. I'm not like you.

ARJUN *(full of unhappiness).* Vineeta probably didn't know why she killed herself.

SWATI. I know that.

ARJUN. So why is Vijay coming? If there is anyone in the world who has no poetry in his soul, it's him? *(Pause.)* I don't like him. He doesn't have true sympathy. At the funeral he looked more scared than sad. Like someone was about to blame him. You know when I punched him for kissing Vineeta? It wasn't because he was kissing her, but because I didn't like him.

SWATI. Leave me alone.

ARJUN. Am I saying anything about you? *(ARJUN thinks about why he is pressing SWATI on VIJAY. It is the poem and the way SWATI is sad.)* I'm a bad person and have been one every day of my life. *(ARJUN burps a long one and laughs both at his exaggeration and at the burp.)* That burnt too. *(He smacks his lips.)* I've licked a rat. *(There's the sound of a car pulling into the driveway, an engine being turned off. SWATI goes to the door. She is eager.)*

SWATI. I wonder if Vijay drinks tea or coffee.

(The doorbell is pecked. VIJAY is there, so heavily padded against the winter that he looks like a football player.)

VIJAY. Namastai, Auntiji.

SWATI. The clouds are like a lid. *(She looks past him.)*

VIJAY. It's already dark.

SWATI. Have the days started getting longer?

VIJAY. Not yet.

SWATI. We only go out in the afternoons. Just to buy food. So I don't know anything. *(VIJAY enters. SWATI closes the door and VIJAY takes off his coat and sweaters.)* How is medical school?

VIJAY. Too much work. And if you start becoming lazy, you get guilty. What if someday you need to know this?

SWATI *(quickly)*. Vineeta was applying to medical schools.

VIJAY. She wrote that.

SWATI. I know. In the same letter. I just want to talk about her. This is the first poem I have ever read, other than the poems you memorize in school. I never used to feel anything with them. This poem I think is beautiful.

VIJAY. Auntiji, I don't know why she wrote about that poem. She hadn't sent me a birthday card in years. I got frightened when I got the card because I had already heard.

ARJUN. Talk talk. That's what the poem is. *(He burps, then explains to VIJAY.)* I'm sick with guilt and unhappiness and it's given me these burning burps. *(ARJUN laughs at his own pathology and burps.)*

VIJAY. Do you want me to look at you?

ARJUN. I'm a doctor, too.

SWATI *(to VIJAY)*. Who spends more time in school, veterinarians or dentists?

ARJUN. Why don't you leave me alone?

SWATI. If there was anybody else in the house I would.

ARJUN. See how she's angry at me?

SWATI *(to VIJAY)*. Do you want tea?

VIJAY. No, thank you, Auntiji.

SWATI. Coffee?

ARJUN. I want tea.

SWATI. You have feet. *(Beat.)*

VIJAY. A little tea. It's so cold outside. *(SWATI leaves.)* How long have you been burping?

ARJUN. From a week after the funeral. Did your mother make you come?

VIJAY. I would have come anyway. To say hello.

ARJUN. Your mother hasn't come. It's been five weeks since the funeral and she hasn't even called once. Nobody's visited us. It's because I'm mean. *(He pulls the hood off his head. ARJUN thinks about his meanness and laughs. The bitterness of ARJUN's laughter can be felt in the way the laughter is brief, contained and inward.)* I don't care about people, but Swati, she is lonely.

VIJAY. I'll tell Mummy.

ARJUN *(sarcastic)*. Tell her. *(Beat.)* Do you think the poem is bad?

VIJAY. It's famous.

ARJUN. "The Love Song of J. Alfred Prufrock." Even the name is, I'm a little nobody.

VIJAY. It's all right to pity, to be sad.

ARJUN. I've used up pity and sadness. Now I'm on to unhappiness. So, is the poem any good?

VIJAY. What do I know about poetry. I don't even like greeting cards.

(SWATI returns with a tray of tea.)

SWATI. You're the first person in this house other than us in four weeks.

VIJAY. Auntiji.

SWATI. Other than him and the cashiers at Foodtown, I've spoken to nobody.

VIJAY. Auntiji, I don't think I ever talked to Vineeta about the poem. It might mean nothing.

SWATI. She wrote it the day before.

VIJAY. For a day after I got it, I couldn't open it.

ARJUN. Who can tell why someone kills themselves?

SWATI. She put a garbage bag over her head. Before she died, because of the oxygen, she threw up. You remember how clean she was. We used to say, "You'll spend so much time washing your hands before you operate that your patients will die waiting." *(Beat.)*

ARJUN. Do you have the book? *(VIJAY pulls a "Cliff Notes" from his coat pocket.)*

VIJAY *(apologetic)*. This is all I have. I only read mysteries.

SWATI. What does it say?

VIJAY. Nothing you can't tell by reading the poem. A young man imagining how terrible growing old would be. T.S. Eliot was twenty-one or twenty-three when he wrote this.

SWATI. Why are the women talking about Michelangelo?

VIJAY. I think because it rhymes with "women come and go" in the line before.

SWATI *(impatient)*. That's no reason. Then it could be anybody. It wouldn't have to be Michelangelo.

ARJUN. Who could it be, the famous painter Mo?

VIJAY. Auntiji, Vineeta might not have thought about all these things.

SWATI *(quietly)*. I know. I just want to try thinking what she thought. Who is the "us"?

VIJAY. "Let us go then"? The reader and the speaker, I think. T.S. Eliot is saying to the reader to come along with the speaker.

ARJUN. I said that. It's a bad poem. It's the first poem I've ever read and I understand it completely.

"Do I dare to eat a peach?

I shall wear white flannel trousers, and walk upon the
  beach."
Then I shall give a little screech.
If some peach falls on my white flannel trousers
Because I have no bleach.

SWATI. Did Vineeta read much poetry?

VIJAY *(shrugs)*. I don't think so.

ARJUN. If she had listened to bad songs all day before she
killed herself, would you want to know what the bad
songs meant to her?

SWATI. Yes.

ARJUN. Your questions makes me crazy.

SWATI. I want to talk to Vineeta. I want to imagine her. I
want to talk about Vineeta. I want people to say her
name.

ARJUN. Talk talk.

SWATI. You want me to be unhappy and quiet like you.
You want me to sit on the sofa all day burping.

ARJUN *(sarcastic)*. Yes. I want to cause you pain.

SWATI *(accusing)*. You do!

ARJUN *(to VIJAY)*. Look at her.

SWATI. When you're unhappy, you want everyone to be
unhappy the way you are.

ARJUN. It's all my fault.

SWATI. Everything is your fault, so be quiet. *(To VIJAY.)*
Tell me, I read some things in the poem and I don't
know if I should feel happy or sad. Deserted streets.
Isn't it good to not have noise? I grew up in Delhi which
is always noisy, so a deserted street is good.

ARJUN. You know what made Vineeta kill herself? *(AR-
JUN jabs his finger at VIJAY and cackles. VIJAY panics.)*

VIJAY. No, no. I talked to her five times in the last five years and it was always at big parties.

ARJUN. It was your birthday. That's what made her sad.

VIJAY. I have a birthday every year.

ARJUN. Don't you remember how on your birthdays you would spend all day together?

VIJAY *(baffled)*. We never did that.

ARJUN. It's him. He made her so unhappy. I can tell from his eyes.

VIJAY. I wouldn't have given you the card if it had anything to do with me.

ARJUN. See, I told you. He has a dark heart from hiding. It's in his eyes. How many eyes have I looked in as a dentist. When people are vulnerable. Their mouths open and ready to confess. I'm like a priest.

SWATI *(begins sobbing)*. Why do you do this?

ARJUN. Cry, cry some more. Boo-hoo. Boo-hoo-hoo. *(ARJUN pulls his shawl over his face and gets up to leave. He burps as he exits.)*

VIJAY. Auntiji, I only kissed Vineeta once.

SWATI. I don't care. *(She continues crying. VIJAY stands before her for a moment. He goes to where ARJUN exited and calls out.)*

VIJAY. Uncleji, she's still crying. *(There's a burp from offstage. VIJAY sits beside SWATI.)* There's a part of the poem that T.S. Eliot wrote and never published. *(SWATI stops crying and looks at him.)* It lets you know that the person speaking is imagining everything.

SWATI. What can I do with that?

VIJAY. Auntiji, Mummy made dinner. I'll leave the book here. *(He moves to stand. SWATI grabs his wrist.)*

SWATI. You are a bad person. You see someone suffering and it doesn't matter. You're going to be a bad doctor. Your children are going to be heartless. When you die, nobody will cry for long.

VIJAY. It's not my fault.

SWATI. It has to be your fault for you to care?

VIJAY. What can I do?

(ARJUN comes back on stage and goes to SWATI.)

ARJUN *(to SWATI)*. I'm alone for two minutes and I get anxious. *(He stands looking down at her.)* It's because you don't know how to laugh that Vineeta killed herself. You made Vineeta like you. If she had been like me ... *(He sits down on the sofa. SWATI continues crying softly. ARJUN burps. To VIJAY)*. You were always a selfish boy. You remember how you came here one Christmas and took all the candy canes off the tree and bit each one once.

VIJAY. I never did that.

ARJUN. People don't change.

VIJAY. You're lying. I never did that.

ARJUN. Now you're calling me a liar. I'm calling your mother.

SWATI. I want to go for a walk. *(A moment of silence as ARJUN and VIJAY try to make sense of this.)* All we do is stay in the house. I want to go outside. *(Beat.)* I'm going to die inside this house. *(Beat, to ARJUN.)* I want you to come. Vijay is taking me.

ARJUN. It's dark.

SWATI. I'm going to go outside and I can't have you be here if you haven't been outside. *(She stands.)*

ARJUN. It doesn't mean anything if you go outside. It won't make you feel better tomorrow.

SWATI. I am going. *(She goes to a closet and opens it. Inside is her coat.)*

ARJUN. Go.

SWATI *(begins bundling herself up)*. You can't be sitting here when I come back.

ARJUN. I'll be upstairs asleep. I'm not like you. Things don't get better for me.

VIJAY. Uncleji, come.

ARJUN. Why?

SWATI. Who knows what'll happen if we go outside.

ARJUN. Don't go. I get lonely alone.

SWATI. Let's go. *(She opens the door and turns to AR-JUN.)*

ARJUN. You want to turn everything into a game. Vineeta died with a garbage bag over her head. With vomit in her hair, in her nose, her ears.

SWATI. I am going.

ARJUN. Go!

END

OH WILD WEST WIND
by Karen Sunde

<u>CHARACTERS</u>:

EDA, a mother
DAWN, her daughter-in-law
RED, her son's friend

SETTING: *A scrim or back wall for lighting. Actions are described in real space, but executed in make-believe space, as in mime, or storytelling, e.g., walking a distance is shown by mime-walking in place.*

AT RISE: *Dark. Chopin piano. Streaks of light. Yells of battle in the distance. DR, two women sleep. Piano segues to native wood flute. EDA, sitting cross-legged on a rug in front of her living room fire, has nodded off while cradling the pregnant DAWN. EDA groans, twisting her head in her sleep; this builds, until she straightens, waking with a shout.*

EDA. No...! *(A terrible dream has waked EDA. She rises a bit, letting DAWN slide. EDA can still see the dream, but is unable to cry out, and clutches the sharp pain it makes in her chest. When the pain and dream pass she's left weak, collapses back, panting, unsure what to do,*

81

sits completely still. EDA decides. She sets her face to hide her pain, reaches tenderly to touch DAWN.) Dawn.

DAWN. Mmmmh.

EDA. Wake. Hurry.

DAWN *(groggy, pulling herself awake).* Is Joe back?

EDA. I had a dream. We have to go. *(EDA begins to hurriedly gather belongings into the rug. DAWN rolls to sitting, holding her belly, sees her hands.)*

DAWN. Go where? Look, I'm still covered with ink.

EDA. Get your things.

DAWN. Where's Joe? Why'd you give me that sleeping dose.

EDA. We have to hurry.

DAWN. Did we win?

EDA. Everyone's leaving.

DAWN. Not us. It's what they want.

EDA. Hurry.

DAWN. They'll take our house, Eda, the cattle, the whole farm. Joe said to stay. *(EDA stops her packing, stabbed again with chest pain.)*

EDA *(panting).* I saw my son.

DAWN. He's not back yet. Don't act crazy, Eda.

EDA. In a dream. Joe said, "Take my wife with the others. I'll meet you across the river." *(EDA goes back to packing. The battle noise is louder, closer. DAWN hears it, becomes frightened and uncertain, but won't give up.)*

DAWN. That's a losing dream! He'll never give up the land. We can fight. *(EDA goes on, ignoring DAWN, until she has all she can carry.)* You're not afraid of a few soldiers!

EDA. Dress warm.

DAWN. I'm not going! I need to sleep.

EDA *(handing DAWN socks to put on).* Wear double socks.
It's cold. *(DAWN grabs the socks, and pulls them on,
angrily. EDA gets DAWN's coat.)*

DAWN. This land is inside us—I can't leave the trees, or
the stream.

EDA *(handing her the coat).* It's too late.

DAWN. The baby has to be born here! I won't go. *(Picking
up her bundle, EDA sets out.)* Come back here! Crazy
old hag. *(EDA keeps going. DAWN calls after her.)* You
can't be on the road alone. You'll freeze, you'll starve!

EDA *(stops, looks back at DAWN).* Your baby won't be
born if you're shot dead.

DAWN. But Joe said...

EDA *(harsh, anguished).* Joe's not coming home! *(DAWN
stares at EDA, has no answer, and EDA moves away. In
extreme distress, DAWN pulls on her coat, gathers a
blanket around her.)*

DAWN. Wait! I have to lock the door. *(DAWN follows
EDA. They huddle, moving away together.)*

EDA. Got to get on a boat. Guns getting close.

DAWN. What have they done to you?

EDA. It's not me. Joe wants the baby safe.

DAWN. He doesn't want to give up our home!

EDA. It's law.

DAWN. Not God's!!

EDA. They make a law that says our home is theirs. And
the President signs it.

DAWN. No. We're Christian now. With a Constitution like
theirs.

EDA. Made of paper? That burns easy. Those are guns you
hear.

DAWN *(grabbing EDA)*. "Keep the press running," Joe told me. "Then they can't destroy us." *(EDA moves off.)* What's happened, Eda? You'd never go without a fight. *(An explosion behind them. DAWN stops to stare back.)* Oh God. *(EDA stops, without turning to look, bows her head.)*

EDA. Our house?

DAWN. It's on fire. *(DAWN watches, horror-struck. EDA doesn't look, betrays no feeling.)*

EDA. Now they can't have it. *(They stand frozen another instant, then DAWN breaks to run back, but EDA lunges after her, grabs on and slides to the ground to hold DAWN still.)* There's nothing to do.

DAWN. We have to try! It's our life burning.

EDA *(holding her)*. Lily flower...

DAWN. ...All your weaving, Joe's carving, the books...

EDA. Don't look. *(They stand holding each other.)*

DAWN. This will kill him. *(Exhausted, they look at each other.)* There's still the press. We can go there. I have the morning edition set—"GEORGIA MILITIA MASSACRES COMMUNITY." If we publish it, they haven't erased us. *(EDA takes DAWN's face in her hands, kisses her cheeks.)*

EDA. They'll chain you and herd you into a pen. *(DAWN weeps, holding her belly.)* I thank God Joe's father is dead.

DAWN. I'm so tired. I just want to... *(DAWN wants to drop where she is, and escape into sleep. She slides toward the ground, but sees someone in the distance.)*

EDA. I know, I know, but you can't sleep yet. Watch for the boat.

DAWN. Here comes Red.

EDA *(alarmed, panics)*. He's a traitor. Come on. Don't even look at him.

RED *(from off)*. Eda!

DAWN. He looks awful.

EDA. Joe hates him. Let's get away.

(RED, torn, dirty, winded, carrying a rifle, stumbles on.)

RED. Eda ...

EDA. We got nothing to say to him. *(RED is very upset. He catches them and grabs EDA.)*

RED *(out of breath)*. I got to tell you ...

EDA. What—"I told you so"?

RED. Eda, I saw. Joe ...

EDA *(interrupts RED by grabbing him and shouting)*. Don't tell lies! *(Frightened, confused, RED looks from EDA to DAWN.)*

DAWN *(drowsy)*. Let Red talk. Have to get ...

RED. You can't leave.

DAWN. ... the Constitution.

EDA. Now we can't leave? *(Watching for the boat.)* That's a new tune from you. Sing it to Joe.

DAWN *(fainting into sleep)*. Is the fighting ... done? *(DAWN slides, she's dead weight, nodding. EDA can't hold her.)*

EDA *(sharply, back to RED)*. Hold her. She's had a sleeping dose. *(RED cradles DAWN's weight.)* Boat's already full. We'll have to get the next.

RED *(near weeping)*. Joe's my friend forever, Eda. *(RED kneels, lowering DAWN with him. She's asleep.)*

EDA *(mocking him)*. Great friend. "Settle while you can," you told him. "Take a price. Leave the land."

RED. Once they found gold here, it was only a matter of time.

EDA. Joe said "If we have laws and courts and schools like them, they'll let us live."

RED. Did I leave?! I stayed because of him!

EDA (*slides to the ground, exhausted*). And *now* you left him?

RED (*stares at EDA, hoarse, choked*). I didn't. Not until he dropped ...

EDA. Joe says he'll meet us across the river in Tennessee.

RED. Eda, listen to me! Joe's ...

EDA (*sharply*). Is Dawn sleeping? She wouldn't leave the press—five days and nights since the battle began. (*RED agonized, unable to respond. DAWN is sleeping. EDA turns tired eyes on RED, as though she's finally ready to hear him.*) Did you apologize to Joe?

RED. Eda ...

EDA. What do you think I don't know? That my son is dead, with a bayonet through his chest? How could I fail to feel that. (*Silenced, RED falls back, staring at her. Stillness.*)

DAWN (*murmuring from sleep*). Joe, the baby ...

EDA. Next boat, little Dawn, hush ... sleep ...

RED (*hushed*). I tried to help him. God gave the land.

EDA (*numb*). They want us gone. We go or die.

RED. You can't leave Joe lying there.

EDA. You want his baby dead too?! (*DAWN cries out in her sleep. EDA rocks the pregnant girl, hums, takes a stone from her apron pocket.*) This is Joe's favorite. From the waterfall. He polished it. (*EDA hands the stone to RED. He takes it, and breaks down crying.*) You must protect those who live.

RED. We should have gone long ago. The whole city's burning.

DAWN *(murmuring)*. Can you see Joe?

EDA. He's far down the road. Sweet Dawn, remember the girl who rode her canoe to the sea? *(Begins to sing.)*

> At sunrise she was far out to sea,
> she knew not where, she had great fear.
> But the wind came to sing to her—

> Wherever you wander, you're under God's sky.

> Trust birds to bring you safe to land.
> Pray the new land will receive you,
> Pray strangers will comfort you there.

> Wherever you wander, you stay in God's eye.

RED. We should have gone in summer. It will storm. And it's too far—a thousand miles.

DAWN. Not so many.

RED. It's too cold. We don't have food. *(DAWN is getting to her feet, looking L.)*

DAWN. There's the boat.

EDA. Come... *(EDA gets to her feet, clutching her chest. RED jumps onto the boat, then turns back to reach for DAWN. EDA hands him her bundle, then steadies DAWN as she steps onto the boat. DAWN turns to EDA.)*

DAWN. Hurry, Eda. Step wide. *(Both DAWN and RED reach toward EDA.)*

EDA. Hold her tight, Red.

RED. We're casting off. Come.

EDA. Walk well down the trail. Take care not to freeze. Look to the western sky.

DAWN. Eda, come!

EDA. I must tend my own.

RED *(hushing DAWN)*. Eda speaks with more heart than she has left. *(RED and DAWN begin to separate from EDA, with little sliding backward steps that simulate each floating away from the other.)*

DAWN. Eda!

EDA. Sing to my grandchild.

RED. Eda can't walk a thousand miles.

DAWN. Joe will be angry at you!

EDA. My home is here.

DAWN. They'll kill you, Eda. *(Drums. March, but with plaintive wood flute beginning low, increasing.)*

EDA. I kill my heart if I leave.

DAWN *(disappearing)*. You can't stay!

EDA. Pray they let you live, in Oklahoma. *(RED and DAWN are gone. Darkness. The march is becoming loud. EDA, alone, turns upstage where a light bursts, but EDA is in darkness. She opens her arms, raises them. Her shadow is reflected upstage. As the march breaks into a military charge, EDA's silhouette grows to fill the whole stage.)*

THE END

ABOUT THE AUTHORS

J. Rufus Caleb *(Slave Coffle w/ Observer)*. Caleb has written for theatre, radio and television. His play, *The Rehearsal*, developed at Playwrights Theatre of New Jersey and The New Harmony Project, is included in *The Best Short American Plays 1996-1997*. His teleplay, *Benny's Place*, received the 1981 Eugene O'Neill National Playwrights Conference Theatre Award for Best Conference Play, and was later produced for ABC television. The production of his radio play, *The Devil and Uncle Asa*, received the 1993 Special Achievement Award from the National Federation of Community Broadcasters. Caleb has received fellowships from the Pennsylvania Arts Council and an NEA grant to produce and direct his radio script, *Moods For Jazz*, an adaptation of the Langston Hughes poetry book, *Ask Your Mama*. His fiction and poetry have appeared in journals such as Obsidian, Shenandoah and the William and Mary Review. Caleb is an associate professor of English at the Community College of Philadelphia.

Kitty Chen *(Rowing to America)*. Chen is an autodidact and the recipient of playwriting fellowships from the NEA (1992-1993) and New York Foundation for the Arts (1989, 1998), among others. *I See My Bones* (1995), developed at Playwrights Theatre of New Jersey, was produced by Urban Stages in New York City in 1997. *Eating Chicken Feet* (1992), also read at PTNJ, was produced off-Broadway in 1993 by Women's Project and Pan Asian Rep and at Kumi Kahua, Honolulu, in 1997; it was a finalist in the 1992 Humana Festival and published by Dramatic Publishing. *Rosa Loses Her Face* (1989) was produced at Luna Stage, Montclair, N.J., and toured with Urban Stages. *Body Parts Trilogy: 3 Metaphoricopsychoanatomical Plays* has been seen individually at Pegasus (Dallas), Women's Project,

89

New Georges, Love Creek. She has also written short plays, children's stories, and a work in progress, *Blessings of Chairman Moo* (not Mao), for which she received another NYFA award. She is a member of Dramatists Guild, Women's Project, and the three actors unions and has served as panelist/reader for the NEA, NYFA, NYSCA, NJCA, and Bronx Arts Council. Chen was born in Shanghai, China, and acted professionally for many years.

Robert Clyman *(Famous Ali)*. Clyman's plays have been performed off-Broadway and in such theatres as the Denver Center Theatre, George Street Playhouse, Williamstown Theatre Festival, Colony Studio Theatre (Los Angeles), Missouri Rep and Mill Mountain Theatre (Roanoke, Va.) in addition to touring in Scotland. He has been awarded a number of national prizes such as the Eugene O'Neill Summer Conference Fellowship, New Jersey State Council on the Arts Award, Edward Albee Foundation Fellowship, and Shenandoah Valley Playwrights Fellowship. Playwrights Theatre audiences were introduced to two plays by Clyman: *Where the Sun Never Sets*, a staged reading in the fall of 1994; and *Sigmund Freud: the Untold Story*, which has since been presented in New York by the Abingdon Theatre Company under the title of *Siggy*. *The Lower Cortex* was presented in a workshop production at Playwrights Theatre in May of 1996, after first being developed at a lab production at the Circle Repertory Company in New York City and was recently produced at the Miniature Theatre of Chester. Clyman is also a clinical psychologist with a practice in Oldwick.

Keith Glover *(A Mule in J.F.K.)* is from Bessemer, Ala. He is a member of The New Dramatist Playwrights Organization and a recipient of a Pew Charitable Fellowship Grant in 1996. His first play, *Dancing on Moonlight* was produced in 1995 at the New York Shakespeare Festival. His second play, *Coming of the Hurricane*, was produced by the Denver Center Theatre Company (1994), at Penumbra Theatre Company in St. Paul, Minn., (1995) and at the Arena Stage in Washington, D.C., (1996). His third play, *Thunder Knocking on the Door*, a blusical tale of rhythm and blues, was produced by the Alabama Shakespeare Festival, Baltimore's Center Stage, The Dallas Theatre Center and Yale Repertory Theatre during the 1996-97 season. As an actor, Glover has appeared regionally at Center Stage in Baltimore as Sterling in *Two Trains Running*, at Hartford Stage as Scott in *Pill Hill*, and as Lyons in *Fences* with John Amos at Capital Repertory Company. On television, Glover has appeared on the Fox series *New York Undercover* as Adrean Franks, and on the daytime drama *As the World Turns*, as Kenny Hathaway. On film, Glover appeared in *Jackknife* with Robert DeNiro.

Meg Griffith *(The Apron)*. Griffith, originally from upstate New York, has been living in Nebraska for the past 20 years. Three of her earliest plays have been introduced at staged readings at Playwrights Theatre of New Jersey. They include: *Scrapbooks*, October 1989; and as part of a one-act festival in April 1991, *Ghost Dog* and *Touch-Tone*. In October 1996, Griffith's play *God's Field* was featured in a concert reading at Playwrights Theatre of New Jersey. Several of her plays have been finalists for the West Coast Repertory New Play Prize, the Circle Theatre New Play Award, the Elmira College Playwriting Award and the Geraldine R. Dodge New American Play Award, administered by Playwrights Theatre.

Sachi Oyama *(Homeland)*. Oyama's first play, *Oyako-shinju: Deathbound*, was read over National Public Radio on "The Play's the Thing" series, produced by Los Angeles Theatre Works. One acts produced in Los Angeles are *Day Care* at LATC, *Boat* at Deaf West, *Kampuchea* at Barnsdall Park, and *The Painter* at The Complex where she first worked with Playwrights Theatre of New Jersey Artistic Director Joseph Megel. Co-authorships include *Tryst*, performed at Cal Arts and *Endangered Species* at Interact. *Yearnings*, a full-length, was presented at East West Players in 1996. *Rowing to America: The Immigrant Project* happily renews her working relationship with Joseph Megel and provides her first playwriting experience on the East Coast.

Guillermo Reyes *(Dead Bolivians on a Raft)*. The Chilean-born author's plays include *Chilean Holiday, Men on the Verge of a His-Panic Breakdown, Deporting the Divas, Miss Consuelo, Allende by Pinochet, The West Hollywood Affair, The Seductions of Johnny Diego* and others. *Chilean Holiday* was produced at Actors Theatre of Louisville, and published in *Humana Festival '96: The Complete Plays* (Smith and Kraus). *Men on the Verge* won Theater's L.A.'s Ovation Award for Best World Premiere Play and Best Production 1994, and has since played in San Francisco's Theater Rhinoceros, San Jose's City Lights, the Seattle Fringe Festival '98, and Playwrights Preview Productions of New York City where it also won the 1996 Emerging Playwright Award and received an off-Broadway production at the 47th Street Playhouse. *Deporting the Divas* played at Celebration Theater of L.A., Borderlands Theater of Tucson and Theater Rhinoceros in San Francisco where it won the 1996 Bay Area Drama-Logue for Playwriting and was nominated for Original Script by the Bay Area Critics Circle. Reyes recently won the 1997 National Hispanic Playwrights Contest with his new play, *A Southern Christmas*, and the Nosotros Theater of Los Angeles' Playwriting Award with *The Hispanick Zone*, which was originally read at ASU's Theater Department and at the Actors

Theatre of Phoenix. He received his master's degree in playwriting from the University of California, San Diego. He is currently assistant professor of Theater at Arizona State University in Tempe and head of the playwriting program. Reyes is a member of the Dramatists Guild.

Akhil Sharma *(Let Us Go Then)* has been published in *The Best American Short Stories 1996 and 1998* and *The O. Henry Award Winners 1996 and 1998.* His screenplays have been optioned by Universal Studios and one of his plays was developed by HBO as part of a festival of new writers. Mr. Sharma was a Stegner Fellow in Fiction at Stanford University. He is a recent graduate of Harvard Law School and works in New York as an investment banker. Mr. Sharma was born in India and immigrated when he was eight. He has worked for extended periods in India for a legal aid foundation for prostitutes in Calcutta and for an adult literacy program in the villages of Rajasthan.

Karen Sunde *(Oh Wild West Wind)* is an actor turned playwright. In New York, she performed some 60 roles off-Broadway and was associate director of CSC Repertory. Her plays have been performed off-Broadway, in regional theatres, on a U.S.A. tour, and abroad—in 10 countries and in seven languages. Her published plays include *Dark Lady*, which performed at the Abbey Theatre in Ireland; *Balloon*, which won three Villager Awards off-Broadway and was nominated best play by Outer Critics Circle; *Haiti: A Dream*, which aired on National Public Radio; and *To Moscow*, which was produced at a National Theatre in Ankara, Turkey, and in New York at Chain Lightning. Scenes from *To Moscow; Anton, Himself;* and *Masha, Too* appear in *Scenes and Monologues from the Best New Plays.* Her screenplay, *Deborah: the Adventures of a Soldier* was a finalist at Sundance, and at the O'Neill Center. For Shozo

Sato and People's Light and Theatre, Annenberg Center, Wisdom Bridge, Actors Theatre of Louisville, and The Acting Company she has written four Kabuki plays, including *Achilles*. She co-wrote the musical *Quasimodo*, produced at Byrdcliffe Festival in Woodstock, N.Y., and City Theatre in Lahti, Finland. For Ken Marini and Cheltenham Center for the Arts, she wrote *La Pucelle* and *Daddy's Gone A-Hunting*. Playwrights Theatre of New Jersey produced *In a Kingdom by the Sea*, and *How His Bride Came to Abraham*.

DIRECTOR'S NOTES

DIRECTOR'S NOTES